The Voice Within

A collection of poems

written by Catherine Turvey

Augur Press

THE VOICE WITHIN
Copyright © Catherine Turvey 2010

The moral right of the author has been asserted

All rights reserved

No part of this book may be reproduced in any form by photocopying or by any electronic or mechanical means, including information storage or retrieval systems, without permission in writing from both the copyright owner and the publisher of this book.

British Library Cataloguing in Publication Data.
A catalogue record for this book is available from the British Library.

ISBN 978-0-9558936-3-6

First published 2010 by
Augur Press
Delf House,
52, Penicuik Road,
Roslin,
Midlothian EH25 9LH
United Kingdom

Printed by Lightning Source

The Voice Within

This book is dedicated to my wonderful Grampy, William Davies, who died in March 2009. He is my out-of-sight inspiration and guiding star.

Acknowledgements

I would like to thank everyone who has helped me to fulfil my dream of having my poems published in this book – *The Voice Within*.

I want to thank my parents, Tina and Jim, and Granny (Sheila Davies) for believing in me and my abilities. I also want to thank everyone else in my family and my friends who are always there for me in times of need.

I am grateful for the guidance and kindness that I have received from the staff of Augur Press.

Introduction

I was born on Monday 13 May 1996 – the only child of Tina and Jim Turvey. My name, Catherine, was chosen well in advance by my parents, in memory of my father's late mother.

I was introduced to books by my Mum when I was very young. I loved those books, and I was reading words from them before I started attending The Grange County Primary School. It was there, at around the age of nine, that I developed an interest in poetry and writing. I left primary school to begin secondary education at Banbury School. I am now thirteen, and I am continuing my studies there.

I find that poetry helps me to express feelings that are inside me. The words and flow of the poems carry with them the expression of deeper feelings that themselves might have no words. In general, I find it much easier to express myself through writing than by talking. Sometimes I use poetry to help me through difficult situations, or to spread an important message. My writing is inspired by many things. These include situations in my personal life, my observations about the environment in which I live, and my interaction with my peers.

An example of how poetry has helped me is when my Grampy died in March 2009. I found it so hard to be without him, and I turned to poetry. My poem *Goodnight Grampy* reflects this. Shortly after writing that poem, I was inspired to write *Angels*. That was the first poem to be published – in *A Guiding Light*.

My ambition is to continue to write poetry and to encourage other people to become involved in experiencing the joy and passion that poetry can release.

Catherine Turvey
March 2010

Contents

POEMS

My Winged Prayer	1
Living Hope	2
The Tiger	3
The Sun is…	4
I Believe	5
Ban Racism	6
Message of Peace	7
When One Door Closes, Another Door Opens	8
Dreams	10
Who Am I, To Die?	11
The Vampire	12
Goodnight Grampy	13
Pulse	16
Angels	17
Steps to Heaven	18
The Lost Soul of Banbury	19
A Victim of Youth	20
Footprints in the Snow	21

POETRY IN PROSE

All Messed Up	23
Sweet Dreams	28
Christmas Confessions	31

POEMS

My Winged Prayer

I'm sending you love and peace,
I give you hope with all my heart.

I will be your friend,
I will keep you safe,
I will give you your wishes.

Let me keep you safe,
Let this angel guide you through fear,
And give you Hope.

Written in 2003, age 7

Living Hope

Living Hope be blessed to you,
Living Hope you deserve.
Living Hope the voice calls to you,
Living Hope for all you're worth.
Living Hope to carry your soul,
Living Hope to light your way,
Living Hope for your dreams to come true,
Living Hope we pray.

2007

The Tiger

I like tigers,
Their camouflage stripes,
The way they stalk,
Hunt in the night.

They're frantically fast,
With a sharp edged growl,
The swoosh of a tail,
A captured animal's howl.

With a drum-drum-drum,
Of a fast beating heart,
They curl in a ball,
And sleep through the mask.

I love tigers,
Fierce, brave attitude.
Just for one day,
I'd like to be in their place.

2007

The Sun is…

A hot sphere of fire,
A burning desire,
A quilt of yellow,
A welcoming fellow.

The soft hair of a young child,
The sound of sizzling heat,
A place of joy and freedom.
But not a very good seat!

Devils fear,
Shining star,
A child's dream,
A place very far.

2007

I Believe

Animals tested on,
Should be set free.
Because I believe.

No wars should take place,
And the world should live in harmony.
Because I believe.

Poor people should have homes, food, and good health.
Because I believe.

Everyone counts, and should share their views,
Everyone's important.
Because I believe.

Let's believe as one,
And change this world, together.

If I didn't believe, no one would care.
There would be no hope in people's hearts.
The world would be fighting against each other
with anger and no soul.

So join me,
Because I believe in you.

2007

Ban Racism

That group over there,
Think coloured people should be harmed.

Black or white, pink or blue,
We're all the same.
Now that is true.

The world is changing,
And so should we.
Don't tease people because of their type,
Let us live in harmony.

White people look down on me,
And shout horrible names.
I don't understand, I have beliefs.
But I back down in shame.

Everyone's important,
We all have rights.
So appreciate each other,
Not end in a fight.

Ban Racism, FOR GOOD!

2007

Message of Peace

Peace,
No fighting, nor glory.
Peace.

Peace,
A wave of relaxation.
Peace.

Why do people go to war?
To be powerful, to have freedom?
Or to make themselves stronger?
Because inside they're like glass, they shatter with every touch.

Why don't people live in harmony?
They need noise to keep stable, sturdy like a wall.
If not they crumble down below, to ashes.

Think of a calm sea.
Gleaming in the sun, flowing slowly.

Relaxation, a state of the mind.

Be happy inside,
And help the world to become a better place around you.

2007

**When One Door Closes,
Another Door Opens.**

The first door I open is labelled *Love*,
Full of happiness and pink hearts.
On my long life journey,
This is a start.

I come to the next door which reads *Friendship*,
Children playing, echoing laughter.
No tear, no pain,
And happily ever after.

The room I enter next has everybody fighting,
A glow passes over them and everyone is released.
I shut the door behind me, wondering,
And then it hits me, *Peace*.

Family is next,
People huddled for warmth round a fire.
Whenever bad things happen your family protects you,
And I'm no liar.

The fifth door is *Happiness*,
The room bright and sunny,
Drifting in the air
Is the light smell of honey.

The next room is *Joy*,
With a chattering sound.
Tears of excitement shriek in the distance,
And whisper to the ground.

Hope is in my heart,
As I enter the next room.
Lots of people are believers,
No fear of doom.

I walk into the *Lucky* room,
The smell of money fills the air.
Someone has just won the lottery,
I stand and stare.

Having *Wisdom* is a good thing,
This room tells me so.
I do not have much time to spare,
Thinking wisely I should go.

Looks are deceiving,
But not always to me.
Beauty is not just the inner soul,
Love is meant to be.

My last room is full of *Dreams*,
Created by the mind.
Things in dreams don't happen in reality.
For now, my friend, goodbye.

2007

Dreams

Your poem is touching,
It reaches for my heart.
I feel sorry that you can't see your father.
It tears me apart.

I had a dream once,
One where I could fly.
My arms outstretched,
Leaping in the sky.

'Why are you flying?'
I hear you ask.
To have a sense of freedom,
One that will last.

'Why do you want freedom?'
Your voice whispers out.
So I can sit on the clouds, ride the wind,
With no one to disturb me, not a soul about.

'Why do you want to be alone?'
So I can see the Earth from high above.
Look down at people from below,
Release anger, I've had enough.

You ask me: 'Why are you angry?'
The way people treat me. I hate everyone.
I just want to live my life,
And then burn to dust in the sun.

2008

Who Am I, To Die?

Our troop is gathered,
In a trench,
Armed for an attack,
Waiting, in defence.

Everyone's silent,
Listening for a command,
No one wants to die,
Too many have been harmed.

I glance around,
Sensing everyone's pulse,
The atmosphere is dead,
Like awaiting an assault.

I think to myself,
Crouched down in the mud,
Of my family and friends,
Blistering stabs of love.

I'm fighting for my country,
That's all that counts,
But I want to be set free,
In my head I shout.

Then I suddenly realise,
I've done my best. I've tried.
I'll be remembered as a hero,
After all, who am I to die?

2008

The Vampire

Once the sun goes in
And the dark creeps out,
Shadows are lurking,
But no one's about.

Then a tortured scream,
Howls above in the night,
His breath on your skin,
Who knows when he'll bite?

The flash of sharp white fangs,
Darting close to your throat,
Piercing through your neck,
Then suddenly you choke.

Gargling, spluttering,
Gasping for air,
When his long, bony finger,
Strokes through your hair.

When you open your eyes,
Everything has gone,
But in its place,
A bloody Dracula song.

With the flap of curtains,
And the whistle of wind,
The vampire has left
When you wake from your dream.

2008

Goodnight Grampy

There comes a time,
When we all have to pass.
Life is a dream,
And long it won't last.

Our spirit is called,
To Jesus above,
We leave others behind,
But it doesn't stop the love.

The body is a shell,
We have to go on.
Bill will never forget us,
His pain has gone.

A loving father, grandfather,
Husband and friend,
Who cared for us all,
And will to the end.

All we have to do,
Is hope and pray,
And Bill will come,
To visit one day.

He has a place,
In each of our hearts.
Now that piece is missing,
Shattered like glass.

Oh Grampy, I love you,
Why couldn't you stay?
To hold us and hug us,
And be here today.

You have a space,
In all our souls,
Happy memories are kept,
Because you make us whole.

Your children are lucky,
Tina, Issi and Jim,
To have had you as a dad,
An angel without wings.

And Sheila, your wife,
Is so proud of you,
You made her happy,
And that we knew.

Bill was a great
Father-in-law,
To Jim and Carlton,
Who loved him to the core.

Will, Ollie,
Lewis, and Ella,
Miss you dearly,
And will forever.

And as for me,
You're more than a grand-dad,
A true special friend,
Now my heart will not mend.

But do not fret,
For we shall meet,
In the clouds up high,
When it's time to die.

Until that day,
Rest in peace,
Goodnight and God bless,
Enjoy your sleep.

Goodbye, Grampy.

30 March 2009

Pulse

When I'm feeling down and things go wrong,
You'll be there to keep me strong.
A guiding hand in the dark,
To lead me straight and protect my heart.

Healing the wounds, as time goes by,
Shining around me, holding me high.
Guiding, loving, sharing the pain,
And that is how it will remain.

For when I fall you'll be there,
To pick me up because you care.
Grampy, please hold me before I cry,
With my head on your chest as you die.

I can hear your heart,
Your beat, your pulse,
Could I have saved you?
Was it my fault?

I'm trapped in denial now you're gone,
We need you back, it feels so wrong.
Help us all and say you're okay,
So the tears can stop running each day.

2009

Angels

What are angels, do they exist?
Laughing spirits, voices in the mist,
Winged creatures, soaring high,
Guiding and protecting, lighting the sky.

As white as snow, as pure as gold,
Serving God, is what we're told.
Holy spirits, from the heaven above,
Helping our planet and sending us love.

Hundreds and thousands, in all different forms,
A guardian is summoned to each baby born.
Hugging and sharing, highlighting our paths,
Working miracles to warm up our hearts.

For the good, the bad, the poor and ill,
Sewing it together, pulling us through.
When the hard times hit, Angels are there,
To give us support and show that they care.

Holding your hand when the tears run,
Lying by your side until morning comes.
So, whoever you are, wherever you may be,
Remember this saying: 'An Angel's with me.'

2009

Steps to Heaven

An angel's voice, soft in my head.
Guiding my spirit, this is what she said:

'Follow me, hand in hand,
On our journey, to a better land.
Jesus is waiting, your time has come,
I was sent from the Almighty One.'

And as we flew into the night-time sky,
I felt loved and protected as the world rushed by.
The stars were shining, it was like a dream,
Silent yet stunning, which I couldn't believe.

'The evil has gone, so do not fear,
Peace is surrounding the gates up here.'

And as I glanced up, light shone down,
A golden stairway appeared, spiralling round.
The angel smiled as I began to walk,
Tears streamed down my cheeks, I was unable to talk.

Standing on a cloud was an open gate,
I wandered in to await my fate.
And sure enough, stood Jesus Christ,
With his arms held wide, to reunite.

2009

The Lost Soul of Banbury

Who's this soul that roams Banbury streets?
Staring through the people that she meets,
Muttering words when passing by,
Then slumps in a corner and begins to cry.

I watch and think from out of view,
How can I help, what should I do?
That ruffled hair and shabby face,
Her world shaken out of place.

I wander over and touch her hand,
She needs to know that I understand.
As she looks up I catch her eye,
Tears stream down our cheeks. I've found her disguise.

She mimics my actions, mimes my words,
This is me, captured, beneath the dirt.
I see myself from a different view,
Who am I and who are you?

She's my shadow who brings me down,
My inner-soul who follows me around.

'The lost soul…'

2009

A Victim of Youth

The 22nd of April
(An important moment in history),
When Stephen Lawrence was murdered,
In the year of 1993.

The Black British teenager,
Was painfully stabbed to death,
Whilst waiting for the evening bus.
So whom did we arrest?

Five people were suspected,
They had a racist cause,
Knew the lawful consequences,
Which they chose to ignore.

The innocent boy from South-east London,
Trying to escape the attack,
Ran and ran, 130 yards,
Bled, injured and collapsed.

So let this be a lesson,
Learn to think and respect,
STOP discrimination,
Don't leave our world wrecked.

28 June 2009

Footprints in the Snow

Soft snow falling,
To the ground,
Walking towards you,
Hearing no sound.

Alone, I approach,
The newly cold grave,
Nothing but mud,
And a whole lot of pain.

Delicate snowflakes
Melting on my face,
Blending with tears
Leave a watery trace.

A surrounding coldness,
And empty heart
Frozen in time,
World torn apart.

I stand there, thinking,
Then send my love:
'Merry Christmas, Grampy,
And Lord above…'

I turn to face
The darkened path,
Head down, walking,
I see at a glance –

Two sets of footprints
In the snow.
One pair is yours,
I'm not there alone.

Although I can't see you
You're by my side,
Walking along with me,
Through these difficult times.

Feeling your warmth,
I'm glowing inside.
'My Grampy's with me,'
I'm filled with pride.

Walking together,
The rest of the way –
A special moment,
To remember that day.

19 December 2009

POETRY IN PROSE

All characters appearing in these three pieces of writing are entirely fictitious.

All Messed Up

So, I've met Paul. He's probably wondering why I've left home, and how I've survived over the years. I guess I should tell him. He could need help in the future. He's told me about his life, and about how Vince beat him. I feel sorry for Paul really. I'm not as badly off as him, even though I have been living on the streets for over two years. My family deserted me. I didn't know my Dad, and I can't even remember my Mum. It's so sad.

I was born in Cardiff, in Wales. My Mum was pregnant with me at just sixteen years old. She was going to have an abortion. I'm glad she didn't. In a way I feel grateful for that. Even though my life has been turned upside down, I'm lucky I got my chance in the world. Two days after I was born, my Mum put me in Radcliff Care Home. She couldn't cope with me at such a young age. The staff there took care of me, and I made friends as I grew older. The children there were in a similar situation as me. It felt peaceful there, calming. It didn't matter who you were, or where you came from. You were loved. But that's when everything started to go wrong.

At the age of five I started school. All my friends from the care home didn't want to know me there. They wanted their own separate lives. I had no one. One day I came back from school and the children at Radcliff had started to gang up on me. One friend decided he didn't like me any more so got an older girl – I can't remember her name – to beat me up when the staff weren't looking. She threatened to slit my throat if I told. When one of the staff asked where I got my bruises, I would simply reply that I fell over at school. Just as I thought the worst had come, my life at school turned into hell.

Billy, the ex-friend that got me beaten up, started teasing me at school with his gang of friends. They huddled in a circle around me, and started making nasty comments about my hair. They called me 'Carrot top', and 'Ginger nut'. That's where my nick-name 'Ginger' originated. This would happen all day every day. As the days went by the number of people teasing me would grow. Some days I felt like crying in the toilets, but I couldn't because there would always be someone looking over the door. I daren't tell the teachers or the staff at home as my throat would get slit.

My lucky day came as I turned seven. That's when I met Jake. I was on my own in the playground when a small boy came up to me. He looked nice, but I couldn't trust anyone anymore. In his hand was a coloured parcel with my actual name on it. The writing said: To Joe, Happy 7th Birthday, From Jake. I stared at it, then slowly took it out of his hands. He smiled. I unwrapped it. In the neatly stuck together paper was a toy car. I was so happy. That's one day I'll never forget – the day when I made my first real friend.

Jake stuck up for me at school. Whenever he was around, the bullies wouldn't touch me. It started to calm down at Radcliff as well. Finally, my life had turned normal. Well, that's what I thought. But my life can never go right, can it? Accidents can happen.

I arrived at school one morning a few weeks after my birthday feeling on top of the world. I didn't know I was going to receive shocking news that would change my life forever. It was the teachers who broke it to me.

'We're very sorry, Joe. We know you're going to take this badly.'

Of course, I didn't say anything. What was I supposed to think? My Mum wanted to be reunited with me or something?!

'Jake's had an accident.'

More silence. Then I finally asked, 'Is he okay?'

'I'm afraid not,' replied one of the three teachers very sympathetically. 'Jake and his Mum were in a car accident last night. It involved a sharp bend... Jake's Mum is in hospital with serious injuries. I'm so sorry that Jake wasn't as fortunate.'

My heart skipped a beat. 'You mean he's dead?' I was in tears.

'Yes, we will miss him very much.'

I was so upset that I ran off, out of the school gates, never to return to school or Radcliff care home ever again. I gathered my belongings together, took some money from the Radcliff's open cash tin, and set off on my journey.

I spent my first few nights on the street in someone's doorway. I was freezing. It wasn't even winter. I hardly slept a wink. When I did wake up, it was around half past six in the morning. I was covered in scratches, and desperately needed the toilet. I wasn't used to this. I needed a bed. I was lonely. Only seven years old and on the streets. I had some money so went to find a café.

So warm… A nice cup of tea… The smell of food… I was starving. I hadn't eaten since sleeping rough. I had found a toilet too.

Once I'd finished my drink and meal, I paid the owner and left. I was going to track down some of my Mum's relatives and sleep there for a few nights. At least I would have a roof over my head again. It wasn't easy. I was walking around all the towns trying to find my Grandma's flat. I was given an address, but that was all. I'd never visited her before, so I had no idea where it was.

In the end I found it. It was near the centre of a small town, surrounded by shops. I knocked on the door, but there was no answer. Great, I thought, she's probably out. I was so tired of waiting that I decided to sleep on her doorstep.

'Oi!' A young man in his middle twenties woke me up. 'What do you think you're doing?' He was shouting at me. My eyes were blurred, and I could hardly focus on his face.

'I, uh… Who are you?'

'Never mind that. What are you doing on my doorstep?'

'I'm waiting for my Grandma.' My voice trembled with fear.

'No old woman lives here mate, so shift.' I did as I was told, and stumbled away.

The man called after me. 'Hey!'

I turned round.

He said, 'I'm sorry if I scared you. It's just I've recently been having trouble with the local children.'

I lied. 'It's okay. I'll find somewhere else.'

'Kid, how old are you? You must only be six or seven. Why are you on the streets?'

I didn't answer.

'Look, if you need somewhere to sleep, there's a hostel on Ruth Close – just around the corner. They'll give you a bed for however long you like.'

'Thanks,' I replied. I walked off and found the hostel.

The woman there said I could only stay at the hostel for a week at the most, and if I still needed more nights, to come back two days after leaving.

It was a deal. I would have food, water, and a roof over my head for free. Also it was a great opportunity for me to make friends. I stayed for a week, lived on the street for two days, and then went back to the hostel again. In total I did this for a year. I made new friends and felt healthy.

But at the age of eight I got tired of this and decided to make a new start in England – Birmingham, in fact. I had enough money and common sense. I'd be okay...

Suddenly I heard the sound of Paul's voice. 'Oh, that's terrible.'

I had nearly forgotten he was there. It was as if I was rolling a film on and on in my head. I sighed. 'Yeah, I know.'

Paul patted me on the back. Eventually he said, 'Carry on.'

Then I told him how I left the hostel, said goodbye to my friends, and went to the nearest train station. It took me quite a few hours. I was so bored on the train by myself. It was jam-packed! Stops coming here and there for people to get off at.

When I arrived I bought a map, just to help me get started. I had no relatives there, or anyone I knew. I didn't particularly want to sleep on the streets again, so I squatted in a house. I didn't force an entry, so the police couldn't move me. I ended up staying there for three years, by which time I was eleven. Then builders came to knock down the building. Back to the streets again.

Some people don't live on the streets for long. They die, or they can't survive. They have someone to take them in. Well, not me. I lived on the streets for two more years. My 13th birthday came. I can remember it like yesterday. I was lucky to have stayed there for so long. I've had drunks urinate on me, not to mention dogs. I've been beaten up quite a lot. I've been mugged, robbed, and all sorts of horrible things you can imagine. But I've coped. It's a cruel world out there. Because of all the stress, I started drinking. It calmed me down. The weather didn't harm me anymore. Nothing did. I was invincible. Then it started to get heavy. I got drunk quite a lot. It was hard to control. When I finally beat it, the smoking started. I'm still at it now.

Then a miracle happened.

'At fourteen years old, I met you, Paul. That's when I hoped my life would change.'

2007

Sweet Dreams

I hate school. It's the worst place you could be in – Brunford High, Glasgow. Nobody likes you. You're just a shadow, wandering the corridors. It's horrible. But the bullies are unforgettable. Taunting you, hitting you, threatening you. I know the rhyme 'sticks and stones' about being physically hurt, but that doesn't bother me. It's the names that cause the most damage.

The only good thing about school is the lessons. You can get high marks and prove who you really are. But that makes it better for the bullies. More to tease me about. 'Teacher's pet, teacher's pet,' the whole group would chant. It was torture.

In every lesson I always daydream, but I still pay attention to the teacher so I can get on with the work and complete it. But I don't even *daydream* normally. If I was a bully I would pick on someone like me. It's quite upsetting really. I'm glad I'm not that sort of person though. I daydream about my dreams. It's crazy, and super weird, but it makes sense. Let me explain.

For the past three years, since I was eleven, I've always had similar dreams, but never a nightmare. Every night I dream about a little girl, around seven or eight years old, called Emily. She's really pretty, not like me. She has long brown hair, about half way down her back, and always wears cute little dresses. She has soft blue eyes – the kind that could melt you below the ground. She is never unhappy, and stays cheerful, whatever event takes place. She lives in a big house with her mum and dad. Her life seems perfect – no faults, no tears, no rain.

When I dream about Emily, I see her playing happily, running around with her friends, enjoying life. I'm never in the dream, because I'm boring Hannah, stuck in reality. In English at school, I always write about Emily, and the teacher loves the stories. I take the class through Emily's lifestyle, and even add in tiny details to make it seem as real as my dreams.

In art, my pictures are always of Emily. The teacher is okay with it because I'm quite good at art. But the class get fed up with it. My bullies are in the same class as me, so at break and lunch they tease me about Emily. It's like hell. They ask me why I'm so obsessed with 'this Emily business', so I told them all my dreams. That was the biggest mistake of my life.

The names they called me then got a whole lot worse. Sammy, the bullies' group leader, came up with the next name. 'Ghost Girl.' Instead of chanting 'teacher's pet', 'Ghost Girl' was the next hit. Because I told them it was like I was watching Emily, that I wasn't her in the dreams, it reminded them of a ghost. That's how I got my name.

In the lessons, I stopped writing and drawing about Emily, hoping the bullying would calm down. But it didn't. That night I was so upset that I ran up to my room crying, leaving my parents puzzled. I never told anyone about the bullying so I wrote it down in a diary. This time, instead of a diary entry, I thought of a poem. It described Emily the way the bullies described me. It's called: 'Mystery Child.'

> There was a girl in a window,
> As dark as the night,
> As soft as a feather,
> As strong as a light.
>
> She stood there and stared,
> Like a ghost from the past,
> Her hair so brown,
> In a night time glance.

The next morning at breakfast my parents asked me why I was so upset last night. I told them I failed a test at school and thought they would be mad at me, so I cried.

'Oh darling,' said my mum. 'We would never be mad at you over a silly test.'

I gulped. I hated lying. 'It's okay, I feel better now,' I replied.

'Good girl,' my dad whispered. He patted me on the back.

'Come on. Go and get ready, you'll be late for school,' my mum said quickly, sipping her coffee.

So I left the house and headed for school, dreading the day ahead of me. Would this nightmare ever change…?

2007

Christmas Confessions

Okay, so how come the Daily West wants my story? I'm not famous or anything. I'm just an ordinary nineteen-year-old boy. My life hasn't been that bad. Well, I've done drugs and been homeless, but it can happen to anyone. I'll still tell them my story if it makes them happy.

I lived at 34, Colbert Street, Lincoln. It was coming up to Christmas and I was really excited. I was thirteen, but that didn't matter. I just liked the season and the joy of it. I'm that sort of person. I like getting festive.

I thought it was going to be the best Christmas ever, until Mum and Dad started arguing. It was over silly, little, petty things, which if you thought about, didn't really matter anyway. But once they started, they couldn't stop.

I thought they were going to get divorced, and I would be stuck in the middle. I hate it when that happens. You're put under pressure to make an instant decision. It's horrible. But worst of all, I can't tell anyone. I'm too scared. There would be more rows if my parents found out that the whole street knew.

I locked my thoughts up inside me. Hidden, where nobody could find them. Safe, alone. Forgotten. I didn't even tell the people closest to me. Other members of my family, and my best friend, Charlie, they didn't have a clue. It was none of their business anyway.

Day after day, I felt myself going crazy. Huddled in a corner. Swallowing my heart back down. At night I cried myself to sleep. The only way to express my feelings was through poetry. One of my most treasured ones is: 'Tear Stains.'

I've been crying so hard,
Onto my pillow,
I can describe myself as a tree,
The weeping willow.

The rain slides down my window,
Just like the tears on my cheeks,
My hands and my body are trembling,
I feel so weak.

The wind howls,
As the night begins,
I might wake up better,
When the birds start to sing.

Poetry calms me down. It sends me into my own little world. No one can find me and no one can harm me. It gave me courage, like never before. So I decided to go and talk to my parents about how I felt, because I was being ignored. But my Mum would just shout at me and make it worse. My Dad would sometimes hit me and tell me to 'shut up'. Then I would crash back down to reality, where my life would never change.

I needed help to relieve the pain. So every night I would sneak out of the house. My parents wouldn't notice. It was like I didn't exist, and I would go to a tramp who sold ecstasy drugs. It would help me with my problems, so he said.

But two days before Christmas, my Mum found them hidden in my wardrobe. She packed my bags, and pushed me out onto the street. I was now officially homeless. It wasn't my fault. My parents drove me into that hole. I didn't know what to do. I found a doorway and slept there for the night, praying that I would be forgiven and let back home.

Early the next morning a middle-aged man woke me up. 'What you doing on the streets lad?' He spoke softly, with a kind gesture.

So I decided to tell him everything, even though he was a

stranger. 'My parents don't want me anymore. They're getting divorced. They made me homeless. I took drugs. I need help.' I spoke in quick short sentences. I was in tears, choking. Gasping for breath.

'Come with me. I'll take you to a clinic.' The man held out a hand. I took it.

We arrived on Gamacil Street, at a mental clinic. This is my new home, I thought. And it was. For two years. I had no visitors, not even at Christmas. No one cared anymore. They thought I was a nutter. I was. But not now.

I was released at the age of fifteen. I felt like a prisoner in there. I wanted to get in touch with my family.

I went back to my house, hoping that one of my parents was still living there. A young woman answered the door, holding a baby, and with a toddler at her side. She told me my parents got divorced and that my Mum died a few months after. I was shocked. I asked about my Dad. The woman went quiet.

'Tell me. Please.' I was begging. Her mouth opened.

'You father killed himself, Liam. Three months before you were released from the clinic.'

I could see she was upset. Her eyes were red and watery.

'How do you know all these things?' I babbled.

'I'm your aunt, Liam. But I can't look after you. I have problems of my own. You'll find your way. You're fifteen now.' Then she shut the door on me.

I stood there for a few minutes, trying to take in the news. Then I walked away…

That was my aunt, and she wasn't living with my uncle. So I was going to track him down. I made a few phone calls and found out the address. He lived in Derbyshire. I only needed to travel by train to reach him.

I ended up living with my uncle until I was eighteen. That was for three years.

One night, when I was still at my uncle's, I had a strange dream. It had to be completed. I would live my life the way it was meant to be. The dream told me to travel to Greece, where I would find my true destiny. So I did.

'Okay. Job done. Thanks for your story. It will be printed in a few days,' said the woman reporting for Daily West.
    I said goodbye and walked into the mist to carry on with my life, the way *I* wanted to live it.

2008